How to Scalp the Mini-DAX Future

Heikin Ashi Trader

Table of Contents

1. The EUREX Introduces the Mini DAX Future

As the German derivative exchange, Eurex on October 28, 2015 introduced a Mini Futures contract (FDXM) on the DAX; it was obvious to me that I had to test the Heikin Ashi Scalping method also on this instrument. Although the Heikin Ashi method is a universal approach that can be applied to all markets, the fact remains that each market has characteristics that a trader has to get to know first. I always find it appealing to try a new Future, to see if I can beat the market with my method.

Thanks to the introduction of mini-DAX Futures, private investors with smaller accounts are now afforded the opportunity to also scalp the German DAX Index to professional terms. So far, they had been forced to hide on either the forex market or on the American mini futures as E-mini or mini-Dow. The large DAX futures FDAX is for most private investors and traders simply too big. This is certainly the case for a DAX index of over 10,000 points (as of April 2016). The derivatives exchange, Eurex has finally come to this conclusion and announced in October 2015 the introduction of the mini-contract.

The contract value of the large FDAX is 25 Euros per index point. Anyone who wants to trade a position with a tight stop of 10 points, risks 250 Euros. Logically, a trader should only try this with an account of $25,000, though $50,000 will be better. The mini DAX future got its own contract specifications. The contract value is only 5 Euros per index point. The size of the Mini-DAX is therefore only one-fifth of the FDAX futures. The minimum price change is not like the big contract at 0.5 points but at one index point. A trader who secures his position with a stop of 10 points risks losing only 50 Euros. In my opinion, he can try this with an account of $5,000.

Due to the minimum price change of one index point the mini-DAX is slightly "more expensive" than the FDAX. But for the mini only one-third of the margin requirement is needed (an amount, which a trader must have available in his account in order to buy a contract). Currently, these are intraday 1,750 euro. The exchange fee is only 0.20 euro per lot instead of 0.50 Euros for the

FDAX. Although the mini-DAX future is still a very young market, it was welcomed by investors worldwide with great interest.

The mini-DAX futures is oriented on the famous "big" contract, the FDAX, the Eurex assumes however that this interest will continue to grow once the international trader community becomes aware of this instrument. If more "major players" would be attracted some movement for the market direction could eventually evolve from the "Mini". On Figure 1 you can see a screenshot of the order book of 9th February 2016.

Image 1: order book of mini DAX futures from February 9, 2016

	8860	6
	8859	7
	8858	9
	8857	9
	8856	10
	8855	10
	8854	21
	8853	29
	8852	2
	8851	1
	1 @ 8850	
1	8849	
8	8848	
6	8847	
42	8846	
8	8845	
9	8844	
7	8843	
3	8842	
4	8841	
6	8840	

2. The German DAX, a Popular Market for International Traders

The DAX is made up of the 30 major German companies. Known shares in the DAX are: Volkswagen, Daimler, BMW, Siemens, Adidas, Bayer, BASF, SAP and Lufthansa. The DAX is by far the most popular trading vehicle of German traders, just as the e-mini is the most popular choice with US traders and the FTSE100 with UK traders.

Almost every trader prefers the domestic index, which is true for most countries. It is a natural reflex. The local index seems to give a sense of familiarity or even security. Nevertheless, the apparent familiarity in my eyes should not be the sole criterion for the choice of a suitable trading vehicle. Much more important it seems to me is the question of whether a trader can trade this or that contract. As mentioned earlier, until the introduction of mini-DAX futures for the German trader the requirements to trade his index were very high. After all for the purchase of a single contract, an intraday margin of 9,000 Euro was required. For the mini SP 500 this is only $2,000. Those traders who wanted to trade more differently, for example, with 2 or 3 contracts needed to have an account in the amount of 30,000 Euros in the FDAX.

3. Advantages of Future Trading

It is understandable and even useful when beginners initially opt for a forex account. With these instruments, you can first gain experience and develop your own strategy. This is indeed better done with small sums of money. Sooner or later, every ambitious trader will have to find ways how they can become a more professional trader. Certainly, with Forex you can be a professional trader. After all, it mainly depends on the disciplined execution of a chosen strategy, if anyone wants to make steady money in the stock market.

Nonetheless, I believe every trader should look at the futures universe more closely. Owing to the fact that here he finds the fairest and cheapest instrument with which one can operate in the financial markets. Unlike any other trading instruments, Futures are traded on a regulated exchange. This has many advantages, among which I would mention the most important one here.

Futures are contracts that are issued by a derivatives exchange. So there is a centralized market, where these contracts are traded. For example you can only trade the mini DAX futures exclusively on Eurex in Frankfurt. Since the futures markets are highly regulated, they are 100% transparent. Each market participant has the same information. There are therefore no market makers, which could chase the future in one direction or another.

Future markets mostly have high liquidity. Spreads are conceivably small too. Also, the fees in futures trading are the lowest you can find. All this features make futures the best financial instruments for an active investor or trader. Hence you will find most professional traders most likely on futures exchanges.

Thanks to the high liquidity, you will hardly ever experience such phenomena like slippage (lack of efficiency in the execution of orders) on a futures exchange. Since the volume is high, your order is usually executed immediately. This is especially true for stop orders. These are almost always executed at the price you have chosen. Slippage at stops also belongs unfortunately to the "hidden costs" that you will often experience in most "alternative" financial instruments.

The importance of good execution cannot be overstated, especially for scalpers. If you need to decide in a matter of seconds whether you should stay in the market or close the position immediately, you do not want to worry whether it really works this time. You will certainly not experience this problem in a regulated futures market such as the Mini-DAX futures. Once you want to get out of the market with one click via a market order, your order is executed. This is an advantage not to be underestimated.

The same is also true for limit orders. If you have set a limit order at a certain price, you also want the order to be executed as soon as the market reaches this price level. This is not a matter of course in most "alternative" trading instruments. But in a futures market you will seldom or never have such problems. Your limit order is executed on time.

All orders and their execution price are being registered in passing. You can view this data in any good futures platform under "Time & Sales". Time & Sales displays a chronological list of the total purchase and sales activity of a security. This way, you get a detailed insight into the transaction history. So as a trader you can observe what exactly is happening on the market.

Another advantage of futures trading is that a future is basically a very simple instrument. Since it is a contract between two parties, it allows investors and traders to open both long (buying) and short (selling) positions. Both parties do not have to bear any additional costs; but they must make an advance payment, which is a kind of security. This is called "initial margin". This is only a fraction of the contract value. Usually the margin is a percentage (e.g. 5%) or a fixed amount.

For the mini-DAX futures you will need about $1,900 per contract in your account (January 2016). This is the minimum a trader must therefore have as an account balance, in order to trade one mini DAX future. If the trader prefers to keep the futures overnight, then they are required in advance to do so. If the trader wants to keep the future overnight, an overnight margin is required, which is currently about $4,000. Both intraday (initial) margin and overnight margin can be adjusted by the exchange as needed (usually at times of increased volatility).

Whether as a trader if you are an owner of a long position (buy) or a short position (sold), each outstanding, non-backed by an offsetting transaction positioning is an open position (called exposure). The trader is, so to speak "in risk".

Since you do not trade a commodity market but a stock index when trading a mini DAX future, the transaction takes place by a mutual contractual obligation to pay a differential amount called a cash settlement. This is the amount of money the holder of the position that has fallen in value has to pay to the holder of the position, which has risen in value.

If your assessment of the market direction was correct, you will receive a stipulated sum of money. In the opposite case, you will have to pay a stipulated sum of money. The holder of the long position (long position) closes this by selling an equal number of futures contracts on the market. But if you are a holder of a short position (short position), you can only liquidate your position, if you purchase an identical number of contracts in the market.

Also take note of the so-called expiration dates of futures contracts. Unlike many other trading instruments like currencies, futures contracts are not endless. They have an expiration date. For the DAX family this is usually the third Friday of the third month of each quarter of the year. Traders in mini DAX futures should therefore always bear this event in mind.

In practice, you will notice that the liquidity decreases in the currently most traded futures a few days before the expiration and increases in the next Future at the same time span. You should also change and trade the next contract. You will often observe increased volatility and occasional erratic movements on the expiry date, which is also called "triple witching" in the trader's language. Usually it is wiser to refrain from trading on this Friday. Finally, I would like to mention the leverage of the futures business. It is mostly significant. A trader should explicitly understand the effect of the leverage. As an example, consider buying single mini-DAX futures at a level of 10,000 points.

Mini DAX futures score: 10,000

Contract value: 5 Euro per mini DAX point

Contract value at 10,000 points: 50,000 Euros

Margin required: 1,750 Euro

Leverage: 50,000 / 1,750 = 28.57

This means that if you buy mini DAX futures, you move more than 28 times your deposited capital. In sum 50,000 Euros. Although this is significantly less than if you would buy a standard futures contract (1 FDAX, value €250,000), you should nevertheless understand that in the best case scenario you can multiply your capital using this "instrument".

Unfortunately, the reverse is also true in the worst case scenario. If you close your position at a book loss of 10 points in the mini-DAX futures you have 50 Euros less in your account. That might sound bearable, but based on the initial margin of 1,750 Euros, this still means a loss of 2.85%.It is essential therefore that you are fully aware on the opportunities and risks involved in trading the mini DAX futures.

While you can trade a future-contract intraday with an account of 2,000 Euros, since the initial margin is 1,750, I would not recommend you do so anyway. In this case you are left with only a residual cash balance of 250 Euros. At 5 losing trades with a Stop distance of 10 points you would run out of funds and you won't be able to buy anymore futures contracts, unless you transfer additional funds to your account.

I made it hopefully clear that such conditions cause unnecessary stress in trading, which usually leads to the fact that you will lose more than win (I speak from personal experience). Therefore my recommendation is: if you have at the moment only for a total of $2,000 (or equivalent in Euros) at your disposal, you should stay with forex trading. Meaningful trading in mini DAX futures in my eyes starts only when you have a balance of $5,000.

4. The Heikin Ashi Chart

To scalp, I use the Heikin-Ashi chart. This chart type has several advantages: The trend is more visible by the visual smoothing of the price evolution (unlike Candlesticks). The strength of the trend is visible by the size of the candle and the occurrence of shadows above and below the candles. In other words, the Heikin Ashi charts illustrate the imbalance between supply and demand very well and even shows the inflection points clearly. Thus, they are an excellent tool to identify the capital flows in the markets. This is well illustrated in the in the mini DAX future example below.

Figure 2: Mini-DAX futures in Heiken Ashi chart representation

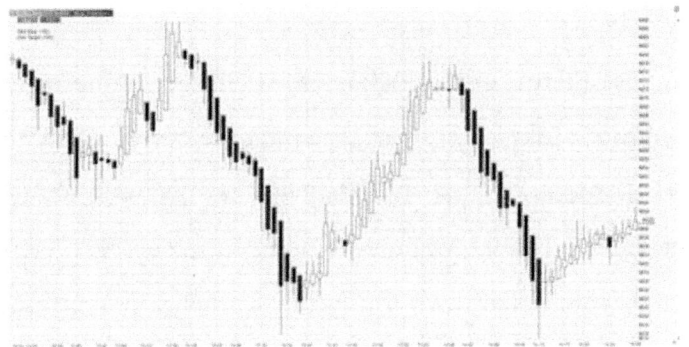

I'm often asked by traders if I combine my method with indicators. My answer to that question is firmly no. Because the Heiken Ashi chart is basically already a kind of indicator. It is a chart and indicator all rolled into one. I therefore do not need additional indicators as a filter for my signals. Of course you can add additional indicators or even other chart forms but I assume that each filter you add to your system only makes the trading-decision harder. And it happens to be my endeavor to keep the scalping process as easy as possible. The scalper trains better through practicing and observing certain patterns that he can implement in trades at an almost unconscious level.

5. What Is Scalping?

Just as there are imbalances in larger timeframes (monthly/weekly/daily basis), which are corrected by the market, there are also imbalances that occur in shorter time frames (hours, minutes) and even in seconds. Here, in this microcosm we find the scalper's playground, where he tries to anticipate the smallest fluctuations in the market several times a day.

A scalper has infinitely more trading opportunities than the position traders or day traders. Since the risk-reward ratio of 1: 1 is extremely low many scalpers achieve with their method, a relatively low payoff ratio (average win in relation to average loss). This is compensated by the high number of trades that the scalper performs. This is called **the opportunity factor**. It is the real strength of this trading style. A scalper may manage his capital more effectively than all other market participants and thus be able to achieve much greater returns than would otherwise be the case.

6. What is the Advantage of Being a Scalper?

A Scalper performs a variety of trades that a technically oriented trader would not make because they do not meet his criteria. Unlike scalpers, traditional traders miss out on a lot of opportunities. For instance, if a falling price just does not reach a certain level of support then a trader misses it by a few points before the price turns back up. The trader didn't take the trade because his limit had not been reached and in such a case, he didn't go with the flow of the market; rather, he waited. At times, this trader may wait throughout the day because the price is simply not turning back (and does not touch his nice support line). Now, a trend sets in which can last for hours, vigorously and without any notable drawbacks.

In this example, the trader missed huge profits that he would have been able to realize if he had taken advantage of this opportunity. The Opportunity costs are sometimes much higher than any fees and losses that come together from trades. Essentially, opportunities are not acknowledged because they do not meet the criteria of the trader.

Unfortunately, the market does not listen to the criteria of the trader; the market itself doesn't even have a criteria. It is a highly complex structure that is extremely sensitive to conflicting and diverse influences. A proficient scalper, who does not act according to the technical analysis, would perhaps have taken a part of this movement and after some consolidation, he probably would have traded the market on the long side over and over again.

What does it take to be a good scalper?

There's no question that the activity requires a large amount of work and focus on what is happening in the market, which is akin to playing a musical instrument or a top-level sport. If the activity of a day trader already requires a high degree of concentration and analysis, then scalping is indeed an art form that needs to be practiced regularly.

The conscious exercise itself alters the physiology of the brain and the body. Thanks to the constant repetition of certain operations, stronger myelination (insulation of the nerve pathways) takes place in relevant brain regions and the gain in line speed is amazing. In a neural pathway, which has a radius of one micrometer, transmission speed is about two meters per second.

Thanks to a maximum myelination, this speed can be improved fifty times over and the final result is a prerequisite for any quick movement. It is evident that this is of tremendous importance to top musicians, athletes or in this case, scalpers. In addition, top performers gain many hours of experience regarding patterns and clues that can remain hidden from the less experienced. So to speak, they know more than others or have a deeper "domain expertise", as researchers call it. For example, top traders know when to trade and when to stay out of the market better than the rest.

7. Basic Setup of Heikin Ashi Scalping

I would like to present an example of the setup that I use when I scalp the mini DAX future.

Figure 3: Mini-DAX Future, 1-minute chart

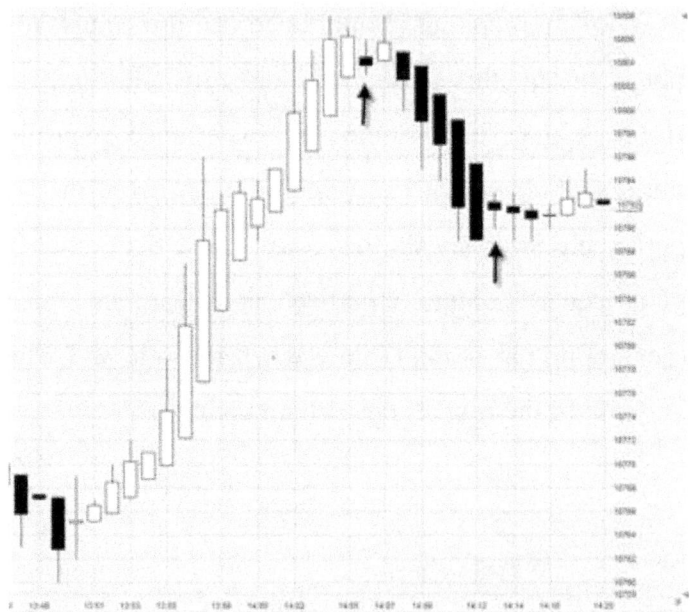

We see on the left side of the chart (Figure 3) a clear upward trend. This is visualized by the white Heikin Ashi candles. Many traders certainly would like to trade those mini-trends trade and invest a lot of time and effort to identify such potential movements.

It is one of the main principles of my trading philosophy, that a trader cannot predict such movements, no matter how desirable it may be. Every trader who is studying the charts of the markets that he has traded in the day must pull his hair out repeatedly asking why he had not foreseen this or that "beautiful movement". It is my firm belief that this trader will in future further pull his hair out on all other such occasions. There isn't any reliable method or indicator that can predict the stock market.

Although the trader is able to occasionally partake in some or even the whole movement. Again, my trading philosophy says that those "successful trades" only must be the result of chance because for every successful trade there are countless unsuccessful trades. For what happened in picture 3 on the left side of the chart, there exist in my eyes no reliable instruments that can anticipate such movements, let alone predict them.

But what happens on the right side of figure 3 (the falling counter-movement, visualized by the black candles), one may very well attribute to Newton´s third Law. This law describes the interaction principle, also called the reaction principle. This means that forces always occur in pairs. If a body A exerts a force on another body B (action), and then an equal but opposite force of body B acts on body A (reaction). This interaction principle is equivalent to the so-called pulse attitude in closed systems. The conservation of momentum is one of the most important conservation laws of physics and states that the total momentum is constant in a closed system. With the momentum conservation law for example the behavior of Newton's Cradle can be understood (see Figure 4).

Figure 4: Newton's Cradle

In relation to the stock market in Figure 3, this means that if I observe a clear movement (upward trend, white Candles) in the chart (action), I can almost always expect a counter-movement (reaction) to the previous movement. In other words, I missed the upward trend, because I could not reliably foresee it. If this motion is clear and large enough, I can expect a corresponding counter-movement (correction). This is interesting to me as a scalper because I can trade this.

The following conditions must be met:

1. The preceding movement should be large enough! In the current mini-DAX future (Stand 10.000 points) this should at least be 15-20 points.

2. There must be a significant weakening of the momentum in the preceding movement (the candles become smaller and/or do not make any new highs/lows any more).

3. Signs of top or bottom formation must occur. This can be long shadows below (in falling trends) or above the Candles (in upwards trends). Or, at the end of the movement doji and spinning tops appear.

Figure 5: doji and spinning tops

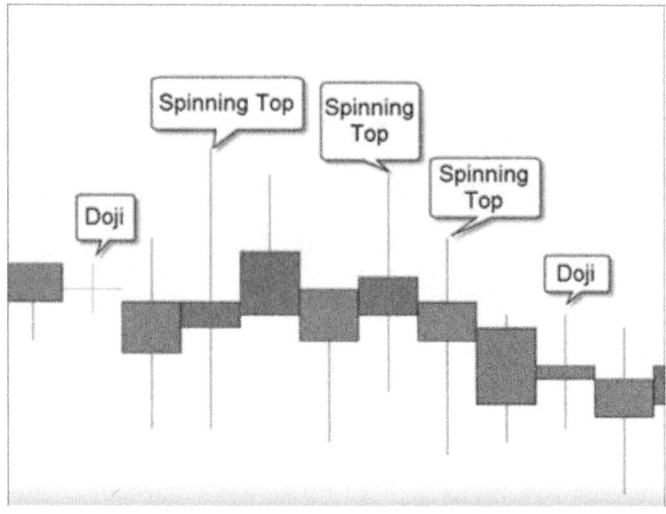

Figure 5 shows some doji and spinning tops. Dojis have little or no bodies with small shadows. A doji often looks like a plus sign. Spinning tops are characterized by long shadows from above or below the real body. Both patterns illustrate an uncertainty in the market. Neither bears nor bulls dominate current market activity. If you then take a look at figure 3, here all the conditions for a Heikin Ashi counter-trade are met. The last white candle formed, if you compare it with the previous candle, no newer high. Shadows appear above the candles and you will see a doji (upper arrow).

If these conditions are met, the moment has come for me to scalp the countermovement (reaction). After the doji I take a short position (upper arrow in figure 3). Although I do not know if this was indeed the high of the preceding movement, but there are at least some important indications, that after the "action" the trader can expect a "reaction". I secure my position with a stop-loss order that I put a little above the high of the preceding movement. Why exactly there? Should the market unexpectedly overcome this high, the setup would be invalid. In figure 3, I was right with my assessment, and the market actually began to correct, at least 5 candles, or 5 minutes on the 1-minute chart.

8. Entry strategies

When I work with the basic set-up, I do not trade with price targets. I assume that the market can correct any length (which it every now and then actually does). So I want to remain in the short trade, as long as the chart produces more black candles with new lows. If this is the case, there is no reason to end the trade, and it is important that the scalper gets those occasional "home runs". Although this was not so in figure 3. Here, the correction was over after 5 candles. We see that the market no longer made any lower lows and that the next candle was a doji (lower arrow in figure 3). For me, this is usually a good reason to close the trade.

Now, the trade in picture 3 is a good example of a Heikin Ashi-counter trade. The setup is clearly visible and the trade could be carried out smoothly. Unfortunately, this is not always the case. The market produces at different levels, daily countless patterns and movements which are not so clear setups as that in figure 3.

In my experience, this is a major problem for most traders: how do I distinguish a good setup from a bad one? This is a point that is given too little or no attention at all in most trading literatures. Usually the author presents his setup using an "ideal" example. That this ideal example in daily trading is rare is deliberately concealed. Thus, the author leaves the trader to his fate.

The consequence is that, enthusiastic about the setup of the author, many traders set out to identify this on the market and unfortunately trade it on good luck. The results are then mostly negative, which at some point as a consequence, the trader abandons the setup as not viable. In order to counteract this shortcoming I would like to show some examples from the mini DAX future that represent to me personally no good setups, although they formally meet the above criteria at first glance.

Figure 6: Mini-DAX Future, 1-minute chart

We see in figure 6 a discernible downward trend in the mini DAX future. Short positions are therefore quite preferable. The three arrows indicate potential short signals, of which I know that some traders would actually trade. Nevertheless, I advise you not to trade them. It is true that there was in advance an upward movement at each short signal. But these were far too small and insignificant that a reasonable counter trend trade would derive any gain. The "action" is, as to say is too weak to induce a tradable "reaction".

At **the first signal** (first arrow left) a doji immersed in exemplary fashion after the upward movement but the first subsequent black candle covers the whole previous movement and even goes beyond them. Who would have taken this bait would have entered the market at a very bad price and would also have been faced with the fact that the previous movement was already completely worked off.

The **second short signal** (arrow in the middle), while following after an upward movement, that seems to be "something" bigger than the previous one, but here, the trader had to wait for the first black candle, before a valid signal is there. The first black candle also includes the complete previous movement. Thus, here the "reaction" is already completed before the trader can ever enter the market.

The **third signal** would indeed, unlike the previous two, have led to a profit, but I would not have taken this trade. The preceding movement is almost non-existent, and moves within the price range of the second signal. That the market then nevertheless dropped further had to do with the falling trend. A trader who would have taken the third "signal" would have realized the profit only "by luck".

None of these three signals would have been valid for the purpose of Heikin Ashi scalping.

Figure 7: Mini-DAX Future, 1-minute chart

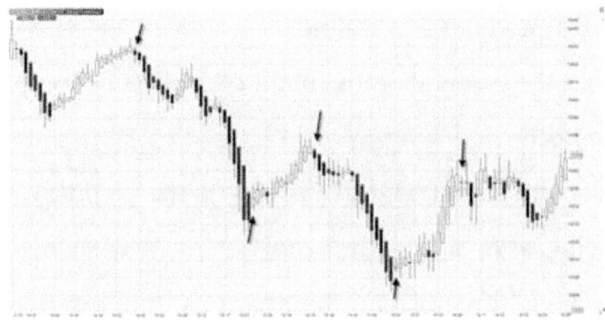

The signals in Figure 7 however, are very well-tradable signals for a scalper. Each arrow in the picture points to an entry signal, which could be traded. Each of these entry signals were preceded by a clear trend, so that after the change of color in the Heikin Ashi charts a tradable countermovement was sure to be expected. Only the fifth arrow (right) on the setup did not work out. Here the trade would become a victim of the stop-loss. Nevertheless, the trader could have earned a handsome profit with the four preceding trades.

I hope the difference between figure 7 and figure 6 is clear. It just makes no sense to trade a countertrend when the preceding movements are too small as on figure 6. It is therefore essential for success, that the trader has the patience to trade only those markets that provide him these clear setups. If this is not the case as

34

in figure 6, it is always better to sit on his hands and drink tea.

Figure 8: Mini-DAX Future, 1-minute chart

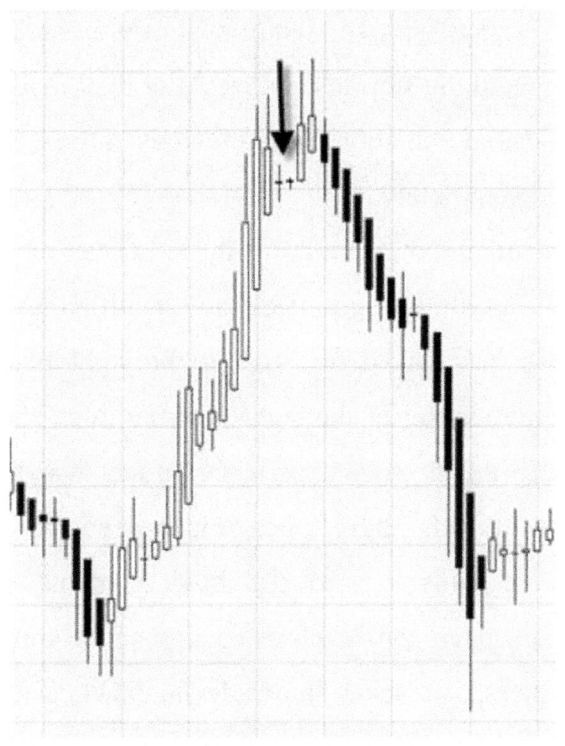

At the end of this chapter on entries I want to draw attention to the above example (figure 8). Here we see a valid setup that meets all the criteria. The "action" is clear and large enough that a tradable countermovement "reaction" was to be expected. After the uptrend was exhausted two dojis arose (arrow, top), which visualizes a balance between bulls and bears. The short signal was exemplary so to say, yet the trade did not bring in any profit, because the market made a new high after the previous signal with two additional white candles and thus triggered the stop-loss order. After that, it still went in the desired direction. The previous movement was corrected completely.

This type of "unlucky" trades is those a trader must bear. He did everything right. He had identified a correct setup. He has placed his stop at the right place and entered the market at the right moment. Yet, the trade resulted in a loss. Any experienced trader will tell you that he still feels angry when this happens to him. It belongs certainly not to the best moments of this profession, having to experience this again and again. Nevertheless, it teaches the trader to practice humility before the market. It teaches him the importance of trading rules and that it is crucial for his survival in the market that he consistently adheres to these rules. One should not forget that such "unlucky trades" faces always "lucky trades", in which the trader despite poor preparation still makes a profit. Again, this is not fair, but it happens.

9. Are Re-Entries Sensible?

An important question, which I have not yet treated, refers to the so-called re-entries. Interestingly, there is on the subject, very little information in the trading literature that I am aware of, although the question of the re-entry contacts centrally the psyche of Traders. With a **re-entry**, what is meant is that a position was more or less "unfortunately" stopped (as in figure 8). The trader is however of the opinion that the setup - after this gaffe - remains valid. So he wants to give it another try at the same place. The "pitch trade" in figure 8 is a typical example. After the short signal, two white candles appeared that took the fixed stop out of the market.

As can be seen clearly in the figure, the market eventually went in the desired direction after the trader had been stopped out. A re-entry seems to be a logical step in this case. At least in retrospect, it seems, because the scalper could not have known, whether the market would now actually fall at his second attempt at re-entry. The example in Figure 8 seems also to be a picture book trade despite the stop being hurt at the first attempt. But we know that this is rather the exception than the rule.

The more interesting question is: why does the trader aim to make a re-entry at all? Since the market just showed him that he was wrong in his assessment. If you get this information from the market, why should we not listen to it? Proponents will say yes, but the trade in figure 8 would have worked out eventually. Surely it would and it would possibly have on other occasions too, no question. But still I stand strictly by the re-entry and for a completely different reason. Regardless of how many re-entries - statistically speaking –a trader can successfully carry out or not, the re-entry awakens a trait in a trader that I would prefer to banish from trading altogether: the desire to be right.

A scalper, who has just been stopped out by the market and then opens the same position one minute later, has a problem in my opinion. He does not "listen" to the market. He wants his trade, no matter what the cost is. In other words, he loses his mental balance and his caution. Above all, he loses sight of the selection of potential trades. One can also observe that it usually does not stop at the re-entry for many scalpers. Often, a number of trades do follow, for which there were no valid entry conditions. In addition, open trades are poorly managed. The re-entry may for other trading styles such as day trading or swing trading be a legitimate means to open a position. For scalpers this is not the case, as the speed and accuracy of execution is crucial here. Moreover, scalping requires a concentrated structure, which should not be disturbed by dubious decisions.

10. Exit Strategies

We have given the full attention especially to entries. Entries are important in scalping. As the examples have hopefully shown, timing and the right setup are mandatory, showing that scalpers should choose their trades carefully. The risk of overtrading and of trading invalid signals out of boredom is always possible. If the scalper manages to select his entries with care, he should also manage his open positions according to specific rules. Once the position is in the market, it moves between the stop and the exit.

I recommend scalping with a fixed stop and not with a trailing stop (a stop order, which automatically follows the price development). The reason is simple. Even when scalping, occasionally, volatile movements will go against the position of the traders. In many of these movements, the position would be hit by the trailing stop. Although the trader would operate a certain kind check in place to limit losses, profitable positions would often be closed too quickly with a trailing stop, which negatively affects success in the long run.

Is the trader not taking a risk that the fixed stop is also hit quite often and that this creates the greatest possible loss? This risk exists at all times. Nevertheless, I have found that this happens mostly with scalpers who have too much "patience" with losing positions. Scalping is a fast discipline. It can be compared to a game of skill.

If a scalper is acting on a 1-minute chart, it makes little sense when a losing position in the market is already four minutes late to take the chance that the stop is reached or not. The scalper should do everything possible to avoid such incidence. The fixed stop may be regarded as a sort of emergency brake, which serves to protect the scalper's capital.

The scalper should therefore not remain passive if the position does not go in the desired direction after a few minutes. On the contrary, if after a few minutes he feels that the trade is a loser, he should act immediately. He should push the stop closer to the current price if this is still permitted by market circumstances, or he should close the position. The second case requires a firmness that can only be learned with experience. It is nevertheless necessary to keep the losses as small as possible.

That's why I recommend not working generously but with very tight stops. The reason is very simple. As a Scalper I am subject to the mercy of my timing. Once I open the position, I want the market to move as quickly as possible in my favor. If it does not or if it ever runs in the opposite direction I want to be out of the market as quickly as possible. If, on the other hand, the market moves in my favor, of course I would like to remain in the trade as long as possible.

These two principles, which may become deep-seated habits only by extensive practice, are ultimately the factors that will determine success or failure in scalping. Unfortunately, many scalpers do the exact opposite. They are considerably patient with losing positions but close the position as soon as a mini profit is achieved. How difficult it is to change those bad habits, I have tried to explain in my book "Scalping Is Fun! Part 3: How Do I Rate My Trading Results?" In this book, I explained the learning curve of a trader who had exactly this problem.

So, it is important to close a losing position fast. How many tics should the stop in the Mini-DAX futures be away from the entry price? This question is not always easy to answer, and of course it depends on the temperament of the trader, whether he (at a current DAX level of 10,000 points – April, 2016) rather decides to use a stop of 5 or 10 tics or something in between.

I'm more inclined to 5 tics for reasons I have already mentioned above. Either the market moves immediately in my favor, or I want to be out. The impact of this decision is also dealt with in detail in the above-mentioned book on scalping. It is my experience that tight stops bring better results than more generous stops.

The main argument against tight stops is of course the volatility. In the current market, the DAX can easily move 10 points or more within a minute. That would be twice my selected stop distance to the entry point. I do not negate this simple fact. A scalper who works with very tight stops will be the victim of such rapid moves against his position more often. So what do I do?

Losses are part of the game. And if I will produce losses anyway and I have the choice between a small loss and a greater loss, then I have no difficulty in making my decision. The argument of the volatility is none in my eyes.

When the defense of the scalper stands, it's time to speak about the offensive - or in stock-market terms - about profit maximization –which is, popularly, the hardest part of the equation. The idea that one should keep the losses as small as possible is what most prospective scalpers understand relatively quickly. Their results teach them this.

How to get the most out of a trade is an issue on which even very experienced traders need to work on time and again. That is also the beauty of trading. No one can predict the future. That is why we are all - experienced or not -repeatedly beginners when it comes to assessing a future market price. I want to illustrate this problem with a simple example:

Figure 9: Mini-DAX Future, 1-minute chart

Look at this example in figure 9 specifically. It illustrates the issue very well. We see on the left side of the chart a clear upward trend, which included 38 points in the Mini-DAX futures. After the high of this move, the next candle is a spinning top. For me, therefore, the condition for a short position would be met. The arrow on top shows the place where I go short.

First, the position seems to be aiming in the desired direction. The next two candles, at least were black,

46

showing a fall in prices but the subsequent candle is white unfortunately. As you can see, the position is immediately at a loss in this candle. The short trade appeared first to develop in my favor, but after four minutes, the market starts to rise again. What to do? If you look at the picture, you could see the answer plainly, of course: remain in the position. Because after the two white candles nine black followed, thus the trade would finally end up successful.

The problem is that you are ignorant of this if you are in the trade and the first white candle appears. All you know is that you have a short position and that the market goes currently against you. These situations occur constantly when scalping and it is important that the Scalper remains clear on the rules.

The main rule when Heiken-Ashi scalping says: **remain in the position as long as the color of the candle does not change**. In this example, we are short, so we are hoping for more black candles. If a white candle arises, buyers take over control for the period of this candle. Of course, I do not know if the next candle will be black again and this one candle remains an exception. Just because I do not know this, I recommend you close the position. This may sound rigorous, but it is important to stick to the main rule.

In the example above, I was "wrong". Finally, the market has fallen further. I recommend closing the position anyway. Nothing can guarantee that after the first white candle others won't follow. So it is better, in my view, to accept a small loss of 1-2 tics, than to stay longer in the position with the risk that the stop is reached.

By studying figure 9 more closely we notice that something is wrong with the correction that we want to short. After the entry (black arrow on top) a candle followed that actually was "none". And the next candle could not convince either, although this candle forms another "low", the real momentum does not seem to come up, especially not if you compare the size of the black candles with the size of the white candles of the previous upward trend, to which we are referring.

The market quite often gives such nice hints. It seems to suggest: Yes, there is indeed a small correction at this moment, but soon we will get started again with the upward movement. It is therefore of great importance that the scalper observes the size and dynamics of the candles and compares them with the previous ones. In figure 9, the white candles of the uptrend are clearly more convincing than the black candles of the correction.

Figure 10: Mini-DAX Future, 1-minute chart

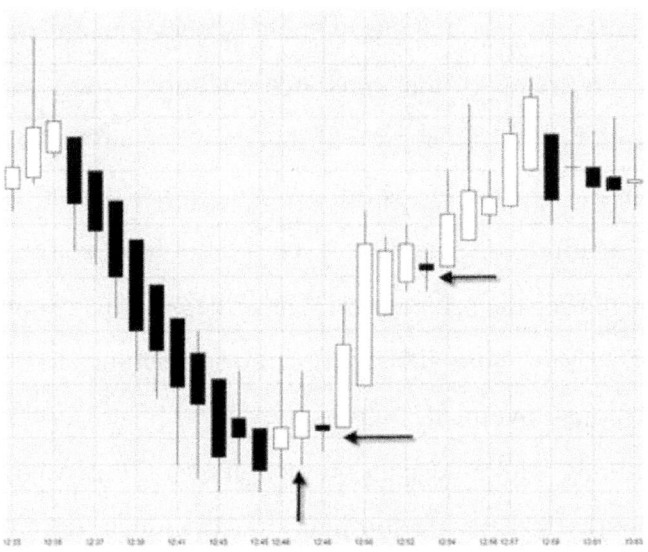

An interesting situation is very obvious in figure 10. Suppose I went long after the downward movement on the left side of the screen (arrow on the bottom). The next candle is a doji (lower horizontal arrow). What should I do? If I follow my own precise rules, I should get out. But in this case, the Doji does not give me cause to panic. The candle is small. Although the two

49

preceding white candles were admittedly not compelling, but in this case I would keep the position, but push the stop a bit closer to the entry price.

Finally, the doji indicates a certain reluctance of the buyers. The next two white candles convinced me then very well, especially the second. But the next ones do not build any new highs, which is questionable in an "upward trend."If that was not enough, a doji arose (second horizontal arrow). In this case, I would take the profit and close the position. Although the market then rose again for 5 candles, I could not expect this to happen after the second doji. Nevertheless, this example clearly shows how difficult it can be sometimes to trade the whole movement.

Especially with a hesitant momentum as in this example in figure 10 there are too many uncertainties that bring the trader into doubt. When in doubt I rather tend to get out than to stay in the position any longer. Of course, the market does teaches me a lesson quite often, but we should know that scalping is not a game of patience like trend following.

When scalping the trader is constantly asked to make a decision which will sometimes be correct and sometimes prove not to be, as in figure 10. Here I should have stayed longer in the trade. Nevertheless, much more important than the points that have been lost in this example, seems to me to be the ability to make a clear choice in every situation due to the fact that sometimes this ability will protect you against greater losses. In total, the lost profit balances the potential losses. Actual gains will be achieved in trades like in figure 11.

Figure 11: Mini-DAX Future, 1-minute chart

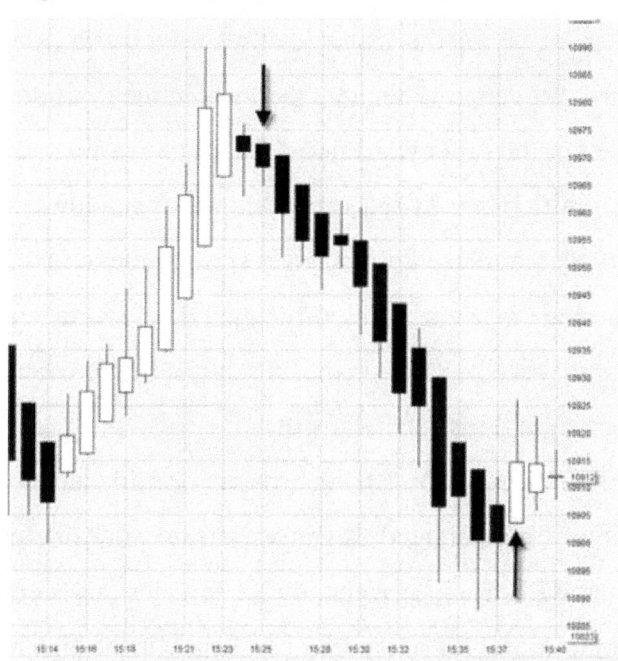

In this example (figure 11) the scalper gets "full loot". After the uptrend (left on the chart) he goes short after the first black candle (arrow on top). Luckily for him, the falling trend is clear. The market forms one black candle after another. Only after the whole preceding upward movement was worked off does the first white candle rise (arrow down). This trade was good for 60 points in the mini DAX futures or 300,00 Euros per contract.

Consider the downward movement in more detail, we see that at about the same level at which the previous upward movement began; shadows appear under the candles of the downward trend. This is a warning signal. Watch out! Buyer! Clearly visible are 4 shadows under the black candles, which suggest that the end of the downtrend is near. Actually the first white candle appeared very soon after that. Finally, this is where the scalper should realize his profit.

Nevertheless, 5 to 10 tics more would have been possible if he managed to get out earlier after one of the candles with the lower shadow. These few more points are important. Of course you can wait for the first white candle to appear. But usually, the trader will give a lot of points back to the market, if he does this.

However, it is not about anticipating the end of the current trend, because that would again be an attempt to try to predict the market. But it is important to notice any warning signs of the market. And the four shadows under the last four black candles were clear signs that the ride came to an end. In addition, the market had already corrected the whole previous movement and had even gone deeper. The probability of a counter-movement (reaction) thus grew by the minute.

Figure 12 shows a classic. After two **spinning tops** and a **doji** the downtrend had ended (left on the chart), the scalper got a long signal (arrow on the bottom). The market rose for nine minutes before the first black candle appeared, on which two others followed (arrow center). For me, the first black candle was enough to take the profit, 35 points gain after all.

The three black candles after the first wave then proved to be small continuation pattern. Some traders trade this sequel and go long at the next white candle. This is not in terms of Heikin Ashi scalping. Remember: we are trading a reaction after the action. We do not trade a breakout after a continuation pattern. It is very important to emphasize this.

Although trading continuation patterns is a legitimate technique, one should understand, however, that this method requires a different "philosophy" of the market. In this technique (trading flags, pennants, consolidation patterns) the Trader goes for a trend. He believes that a once established trend will continue. This happens every now and then, especially during strong trend days. Therefore, this technique works on these days very well. Unfortunately, trend days are the exception rather than the rule. In general, the markets go sideways and early trends are corrected. That's why I rely on the counter trend technique of Heikin Ashi Scalping. In the majority of cases this setup is more accurate. Should a trader who has identified a trend day, change the method and rely on continuation pattern? This question of course can only be answered individually. Nevertheless, I want you to consider that most traders I know are overburdened with the simultaneous use of multiple techniques.

Most of the times, it is better to master one method and stick to it. The results are then usually better. The disadvantage of this approach is that the trader will not perform that well on trend days. But, that is part of the game.

11. Are Multiple Targets Sensible?

A hot topic, even for a scalper, is the use of multiple targets. In this technique, the trader does not try to determine one target price, but several. This works of course only if he trades more than one future contract. Based on the Mini DAX future this could mean, for example, that the target price for the first contract would be 10,250, for the second contract at 10,260, and so on.

The question, every scalper must ask himself is, whether he has the time to deal with such complex exit strategies. For a day trader or a swing trader multiple targets could be an interesting extension of their trading method. When I scalp I keep it as easy as possible. If the Heikin Ashi candles give a clear signal that I should get out, I close in general all contracts. If you are short, for example, with two contracts and a bullish candle appears that could start a countermovement, it is in my view to better close the full position. If you still have a contract in the market, where is the target for this?

It could be, of course, that the market, in spite of a bullish candle continues to fall and that the second contract is closed at an even greater gain than the first. But that is far from certain. Often the opposite happens, and you have to be satisfied with a smaller profit to the second contract. That would not be in the sense of maximizing profits.

However, I would rather have a neutral look at the possibility of scalping with multiple targets. There are scalpers, who are very successful with it. But keep in mind that it takes experience to successfully apply this method. I would not want to see it as an advanced stage of my setup. For some traders, this technique has a more psychological effect. Of course, it satisfies the ego (and the need for security) to take "some profit" on the way to the target. In contrast, there is no objection to this; the solution however, seems to me suboptimal in the sense of maximizing profits.

12. When You Should Scalp the Mini-DAX-Future (and When Not)

Do you know the ultimate secret to the stock market? No? There is no particular strategy or trick. It is certainly not a specific indicator and it is not a hidden market, known only to the initiated. The most underrated secret is, knowing when you should go to the market and when not. This issue was so important to me that I even wrote a book about it: "Trading is Flow Business". You can find it on Amazon.

The best time to scalp the DAX is a well known fact. It is the European morning, 09:00 to 12:00 CET or 08:00 to 11:00 GMT for British Traders. This is the time when the Europeans are "among themselves". Asian and Australian traders have ended their trading at this time and the Americans are still in bed (mostly).

In my experience you will find here the best conditions to trade the mini-DAX futures. If you familiarize yourself with the movements that take place here, you will have a good chance to trade the DAX successfully. While the DAX is not an easy market, it provides a trader sufficient volatility on an almost daily basis so there is always something to trade. The mini-movements that I have shown in the above examples will be seen constantly here, so there are enough opportunities to scalp. And the newly introduced contract Mini DAX futures are the ideal tool to do this professionally.

Whether you should scalp the **pre-market** (8:00 a.m. to 9:00 CET) depends in my opinion, on your experience. Keep in mind that the market often opens with a gap and this requires sometimes a new orientation for traders that already have a position. Precisely because of the lower liquidity the pre-market can sometimes be very profitable. On the other hand the execution of orders can be poorer.

Of course, you can scalp the mini-DAX futures in the **European afternoon** (US morning session). However, you must take into consideration that from 08:00 am (EST) American traders enter the market and mostly they have their own agenda. Rarely, the tendency of the European morning is completely overturned and the opposite of what you saw in the morning trade happens. Hence, I prefer to trade the American futures and return the next morning back to the DAX. But staying in the

DAX can be a profitable alternative for a trader, if looking for fewer competitors than in the US futures.

Avoid scalping when important economic news is published. The trader should therefore scrutinize the economic calendar on a daily basis before starting the day. I would also recommend closing positions a few minutes before the release of the news. I would also not go in the market in the first minutes after the release. Observe what is happening and wait for a good setup.

In the hours before important events such as the **interest rate decisions** of the central banks (and the subsequent press conferences) you will often experience that the market is listless and swings sideways indecisively. Typically, you will find there are very few or no good setups. It often becomes much more volatile then as soon as the press conference starts (08.30 EST in the rule for the ECB). Often it is better to wait for this event while drinking a cup of tea (or coffee like I do).

13. Useful Tools for Scalpers

Although scalping is not a market making in the true sense, this trading style contributes much to the liquidity of the order book. Scalpers thus follow other traders and investors that their orders are executed on better terms. Even if that is not their trading destination, it is still their function in the world of stock market. Conversely, this means, of course, that scalpers depend to open and manage their orders on the most advanced technology that is available. The rapid and efficient execution of the order management supports the scalper in his effort to precision.

As I have already stated on several occasions elsewhere, when scalping each tic or pip counts. Each point, each tic it wins by accuracy, increases its profitability or makes it possible. This becomes perhaps not noticeable at a single trade. But if you perform hundreds of trades per week or per month, a single point more or less can make a big difference. It can ultimately make the difference between a profitable or non-profitable business. Even though the scalper performs many trades, a tick more or less is important. When the scalper affords an inaccurate execution on a single trade this is certainly not the end. However, if he performed thousands of trades every month, then a tic more is pure cash in a futures market as the Mini-DAX.

In order to achieve this level of professionalism, the scalper should have access to the most advanced instruments that he can find in the market. The use of these instruments when scalping optimizes his efficiency in daily trading considerably. The most advanced platform that I know of is the **NanoTrader** of the Luxembourg **Broker WHSelfinvest**. This platform has all the necessary tools and instruments to scalp efficiently the mini DAX futures. I want to introduce one of the most important features of this platform here.

A. Placing Orders

Figure 13: Placing orders out from the order book

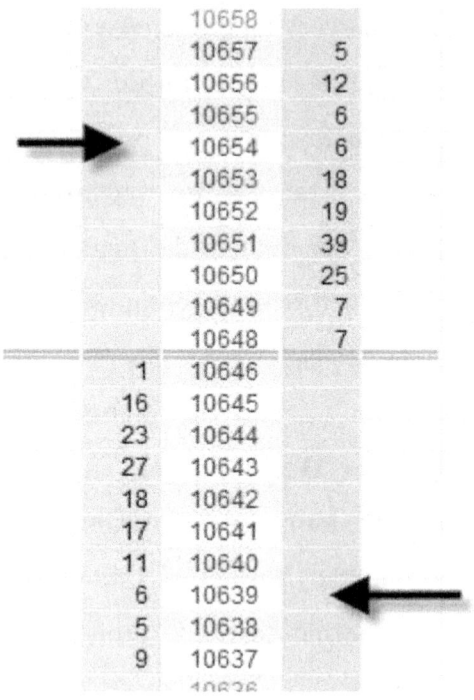

	10658	
	10657	5
	10656	12
	10655	6
	10654	6
	10653	18
	10652	19
	10651	39
	10650	25
	10649	7
	10648	7
1	10646	
16	10645	
23	10644	
27	10643	
18	10642	
17	10641	
11	10640	
6	10639	
5	10638	
9	10637	
	10636	

The order book is as the "point of sale" of a market. It is the place where buyers and sellers come together and agree on a price. In modern futures markets such as the Mini-DAX future there are only electronic order books. Here above you can see a screenshot of the Mini-DAX order book of 23rd December, 2015.

In the **left column** you see the **BIDs**. This is the list of the number of contracts the buyers are willing to buy at a certain price. At the current price of 10646 at the time of recording only 1 buyer was willing to buy 1 contract. For the next best price of 10645, buyers were however willing to buy 16 contracts.

In the **right column** you will see the **ASKs**. This is a listing of the number of contracts sellers are willing to sell at a certain price. For current lowest asking price of 10648, sellers were willing to sell 7 contracts.

By right-clicking in the **left column** (the Bid), the scalper can put a buy stop at the price of 10654 (left arrow). If he wants to buy directly to the current market price he can do this with a left-click buy order. In this case, this would be in the left column next to the number 10648. Then he buys at the price of one or more contracts of the 7 offered. Does he expect that the market will fall a little further, he could of course with a left-click in the left column put a limit buy position, for example at the price of 10,641.

If he wants to sell it, he can do so directly at the market price with a left-click in the **right column** (the Ask). He would then sell a contract to the buyer at the price of

10646. If he wants to sell at a lower price, he could do this with a sell stop at the price of 10639 (arrow bottom right). He can also place a limit sell order at a higher price by left-clicking, for example at the price of 10655.

Unlike other scalping methods, the observation of the order book is not mandatory with Heikin Ashi scalping. However, it has the advantage that all the information of the market is available to the scalper on which he can then react with a simple mouse click.

B. Open and Close Orders

Figure 14, open and close orders

Position Size:	10758	
1	10757	
Position Price	10756	
10729	10755	
	10754	
P/L:	10753	
20.00	10752	
Last:	10751	
10733	10750	
Order Volume:	10749	
1	10748	
	10747	
Buy 1 Market	10746	
Sell 1 Market	10745	2
	10744	2
+1 -1	10743	3
	10742	3
↻ x 2	10741	7
Close & Cancel	10740	8
	10739	43
Cancel All	10738	21
Cancel Asks	10737	4
Cancel Bids	10736	6
	10735	
Auto Ask	1	10734
	3	10733
Auto Bid	20	10732
	14	10731
	6	10730
	19	10729
	7	10728
	9	10727
	16	10726
	7	10725

In Figure 14, I bought with a single click in the order book a contract in the mini-DAX futures at a price of 10729 (arrow). As the market has now risen further (currently at 10733 points, left corner of the image) I had at the moment of the screenshot a small book gain of 4 tics, i.e. 20 Euros. However, the platform provides for the opening and closing of orders a number of other functions. The scalper can buy or sell with one click via market order (on the left, under Order Volume: Buy 1 Market, Sell 1 Market).

The buttons "+1", "-1" and "x2" allow scalpers to increase the contract amount. The little arrow below the "+1" button allows him to turn the position. Here, the current position is automatically closed and the inverted position is opened.

The button "Close and Cancel" closes the current position and cancels all outstanding orders. The button "Cancel Asks" cancels all orders in the Ask and the button "Cancel Bids" cancels all orders in the Bid. With the button "Auto Ask" the scalper can even put a sell limit at the ask price, and with the "Auto Bid" button put a buy-limit on the bid price.

C. Managing Open Orders

Figure 15: managing open orders

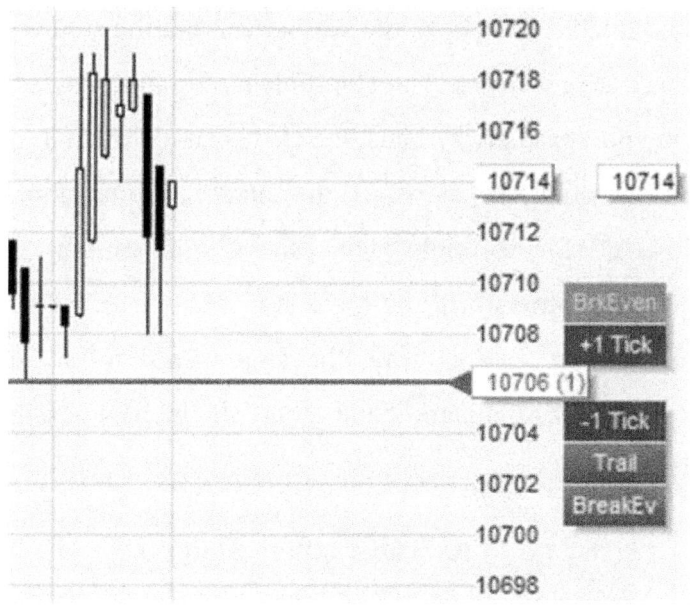

When the position is in the market, managing of the open orders that accompany the position starts. As an example (Figure 15) you see a stop order to protect a long position. The long position was opened at 10714 and was accompanied by a stop (horizontal red line in the chart). The stop is currently at a price of 10706, i.e. 8 tics deeper. The scalper now has different ways to manage the stop order. He can increase or decrease the stop thanks to a tactic tool (bottom right of the screen next to the price) by clicking one tick (+1 tick button, -1 tick button).

If the trade is at a profit the scalper can put the stop with a click at breakeven. The stop thus moves automatically to the purchase price. Thus, the trade can never go in the loss direction anymore. If the market circumstances allow it (for example, with strong momentum) the scalper can transform the fixed stop with one click to a trailing stop. In this way, the stop would follow the momentum of the market and secure the highest possible profits.

D. The Trailing Stop

Figure 16: The trailing stop as profit maximization tool

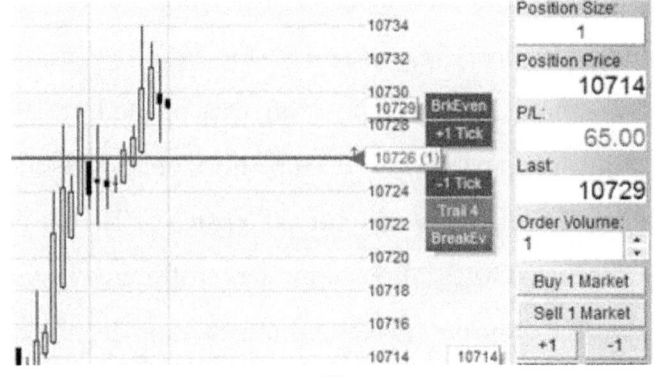

The conversion of a fixed stop to a trailing stop was possible in the above example (figure 15). After the position was 15 pips in profit with a mouse click I activated the trailing function and set it to 4 ticks distance to the current price (now at 10726). Thus, I did not close the position yet but ensured that only a little profit would be returned to the market. However, the trailing stop allows further gains if the market should continue to rise. This feature is especially meaningful at the end of a strong trend because in this case it comes to bring the harvest safely to the barn.

All these functions serve to support the scalper with **profit maximization** and **loss minimization**. As already said, it really depends on each single tic. The more tics you can save, thanks to the sophisticated technology in the mini DAX futures, the higher your profits will go.

14. Various Stop-Orders

Scalpers, who take their trading style seriously, sooner or later have no choice but to reflect on the issue "stop". The stop order has essentially two functions. You can open a position (stop buy or stop sell) and close a position automatically when a certain price level is reached in the market.

The second function is so important because it protects your position in front of a larger capital loss. Stops are therefore important tools of risk management. In addition to protecting the capital, the protective stop can also execute a very different function, namely the protection of accrued profits. First, the scalper should set the stop order to breakeven (to the entry price) so that the trade can no longer go in the loss. The function of profit-protection to the stop order becomes, of course, if the scalper moves the stop with increasing profit manually higher (in case of a long position) and thus ensures more and more profit.

Now, there is no objection to moving the stop manually. For day traders or swing traders, this should not be a problem. These traders can use swing levels in a trending market to do this. Scalpers on the other hand, who are usually dealing with fast markets, should use more professional instruments, not least because they give them an advantage over the competition.

I would like to present some **automated stop orders**, offered by the broker **WHSelfinvest** on its platform **NanoTrader**. These stop orders are designed specifically for trading and scalping in fast markets. They are therefore an important contribution to the scalper's tools of trade. Of course you can scalp without these tools but why should I give up tools that give me a clear advantage over other market participants?

A. The fixed stop

The fixed stop is something every trader knows. It's the classic stop-loss order, which serves to limit the loss of the open position from the beginning onwards. If the scalper open a long position in the mini DAX futures at 10,200 points, he can set a fixed stop at 10,990 points, the position is automatically closed when the market falls 10 points. This stop, as its name expresses, remains firm and stays in the market until the trader cancels the order or the market reaches this price level. Nevertheless, the trader can at any time move the fixed stop. He could move it, for example, 5 points higher at 10,195, once the market has risen by 5 points (to 10,205).

I prefer this method. I would like the mini DAX futures going in my direction as soon as I open a position. If this is the case, I begin to minimize the risk. If the Mini DAX future rises further to 10,210 points I would put the firm stop to breakeven. So I'm sure that whatever happens now, I will suffer no loss on this trade. I attribute this measure to good trading habits.

The scalper can also move the fixed stop further upwards (or down with short positions, should the market continue to rise. Thus, the scalper secures at least a portion of the accrued capital gains. Eventually, the stop will be hit by the market and the position will be closed automatically. In many cases, the manual managing of the fixed stop is sufficient. Nevertheless, the scalper should be familiar with semi-automatic stop functions.

B. The Trailing Stop

If the scalper does not want to manage the stop manually, he may have an alternative in the trailing stop. We have mentioned this stop in the previous chapter. Once the market moves in the desired direction, the trailing stop automatically follows at a specified distance. This distance may be fixed by the trader at will. If the market moves temporarily in the other direction, however, the trailing stop will stop at the last level until the market moves again in the desired direction. The trailing stop moves only a point further if the previous level is exceeded.

The advantage of a trailing stop is that he, unlike the fixed stop, can also rise automatically above the entry price, should the market rise higher than the distance between entry and the originally specified trailing stop. The trailing stop then continues to follow the market price as long as it is running in the desired direction. The trailing stop thus has two functions. On one hand, it limits the loss by following the market price once it is running in the desired direction. On the other hand, it ensures the book profit when the market price continues to go in favor of the trader.

The Trailing Stop, thus, automates **the position management** and makes the manual pushing of fixed stops unnecessary.

If the trailing stop for certain trading strategies is very suitable, it can be used only conditionally for scalping. The reason is the unpredictable volatility in the micro range of scalping. It is difficult to determine a fixed value at which the trailing stop can be of "optimal" use. At least with "normal scalping" I could hitherto see no added value for the use of a trailing stop. Too often the position was taken out of the market by the trailing stop, whereas it would not even have been bound by the observation of the Heikin Ashi charts.

The trailing stop has proven its value with positions that were already far in profit (as in figure 16). In the mini DAX future, these are mostly book gains of 20 points or more. Here I use at the (estimated) end of the movement a trailing stop at a small distance at the current market to get the most out of the move. Of course, these scalp trades are the highlights of the week. Unfortunately, they occur only occasionally. But, they improve the weekly performance significantly.

C. The Linear Stop

Figure 17: The Linear Stop

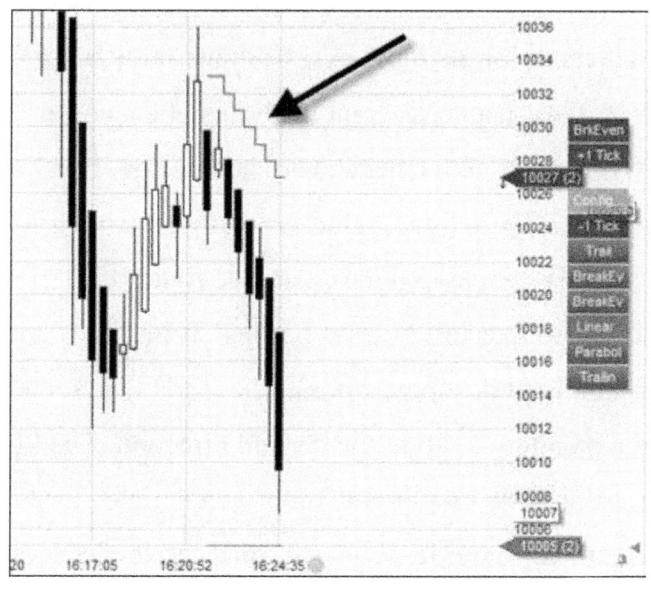

A very different kind of stop is the linear stop, and as far as I know; only the broker WHSelfinvest offers this option. Unlike the trailing stop the linear stop does not follow the market price, but is drawn for each period at a certain distance. If a trader is scalping the mini DAX future based on the 1-minute chart the linear stop could be tightened, for example every minute by a factor of 2 points. This happens completely independent of the current market movement. The linear stop rises with each period by a fixed value. Therefore the stop looks like a small staircase on the chart (see figure 17).

I personally like this feature because it highly supports my scalping philosophy. I prefer the market, as soon as I open a position, to go in the desired direction. The linear stop brings an important time factor into the stop management. Experience teaches that the longer it takes for a position to get in the win, the less likely this scenario will occur.

The linear stop supports me automatically in this attempt. This is especially important if the market goes sideways for several minutes and the anticipated movement does not really pick momentum. Then, I like to have a stop which automatically gets me out the market after a few periods (minutes). In other words: the linear stop helps me in my efforts to achieve discipline!

D. The Time Stop

The more radical version of a linear stop is the time stop. As the name suggests, the time stop works with a time limit. It automatically closes the position after an advanced set number of periods, regardless of how the market has developed within this period. This initially sounds like a very rigorous measure, but again, experience shows that a trade whose expected scenario is not honored after a certain time is better closed in most cases, regardless of whether profit or loss is made.

A scalper in the mini DAX future might have made the experience, for example, that most of its profit positions were closed after less than 8 minutes. Would it not be useful to automatically install this period of limitation in the system? Of course, scalpers should experiment beforehand with this function before they actually implement it into its system.

But the advantages of this stop type are obvious in my view, precisely in the fast scalping game. In addition, this stop closes the position at the market price. Thus, the market does not have to come back (and therefore eat the profits of the trader). Of course there is a risk that the trade closes too early and potential gains are not realized. Here, of course, the trader could take the time Stop from the market and replace it by another stop type. A warning must however be pronounced. Since the time Stop has no fixed set price level it naturally carries unlimited risk in itself. Therefore, he must always be combined with at least one additional stop function, so this scenario does not occur. This could for example be a fixed stop or a trailing stop.

E. The Parabolic Stop

Figure 18: Parabolic Stop

A particularly sophisticated alternative is the parabolic stop. The name already says what this stop is all about. This Stop gets, when it comes to fruition, the shape of a parabola. The number of periods, the degree of tilt and the maximum gradient is specified in advance by the trader. Of course, here, some practice on a demo account is required until the scalper find the optimal setting for the Mini-DAX futures.

The idea behind this feature is that a market movement sometime takes momentum and the price development over time "accelerates". This situation is what the parabolic stop tries to catch by being tightened and accelerated by a factor of the slope, till the maximum slope is reached. It is therefore good for fast movements, which is precisely the field of a scalper.

F. Combining Stop Orders

It is a special characteristic of the NanoTrader of the broker WHSelfinvest, that it has an open architecture. Countless functions to other words can be combined together and linked. The scalper can exploit this advantage by optimizing his exit strategy by trying to get the best of all worlds. The presented stop orders can all be combined. One example I already mentioned is the disadvantage of the time stop (unlimited risk) which can be neutralized by a simple link to a fixed stop.

But even more interesting combinations are conceivable. The scalper can link the trailing Stop with a time stop. In a sideways movement in the market the trailing stop pauses at a certain level. If this trailing stop was combined with a time stop, this closes the position at the market price before it falls back to the level of the trailing stop.

G. Multiple Stops and Multiple Targets

The NanoTrader is the only trading platform that allows you to get in and out of the market in several steps. If, for example, the trader is 3 contracts long at a price of 9000 points in the mini DAX future, he could set for each contract a different sell order. As an example:

Contract 1 target: 9010

Contract 2 target: 9015

Contract 3 target: 9020

Suppose the target price for contract 1 has been reached the trader is now long 2 contracts, with respective price targets of 9015 and 9020. The stop order then adjusts accordingly to the remaining contracts.

15. On the Stock Exchange Money Is Made with Exit Strategies!

I hope that with this digression on the various stop functions available to the traders nowadays I could show the possibilities, thanks to modern technology available. Ultimately, it is always a question of developing the exit strategy that best fits the method and the personality of the scalper. Many will keep at a fixed stop, but other traders could take advantage of a linear or a parabolic stop. Again, nothing is set in stone. It is also possible that advanced traders combine different stop functions depending on market conditions. The aim should always be to optimize the profit and reduce the loss.

Even very experienced traders do not stop to learn. Exit strategies belong to the most difficult part of the trading business. Finally, here, the money is made although it is not with the entries, which the vast majority of beginners think. **An efficient exit method** must eventually be worked out by each trader himself. A book like this can only offer suggestions. A definitive statement of how and when a position is to close cannot be given here. Each market situation is different and the internal structure of the markets is constantly changing.

A trader or scalper is therefore someone who works permanently on his exit strategy. It is crucial that the trading tools will eventually automatically be used by the scalper. The whole focus then applies to market activity and not to technology. Only the actions that you can perform almost unconsciously, because you have already done it so often can be considered as real experience. Experienced traders no longer have to think about how to secure a winning position by subsequently moving a stop or the insertion of a trailing stop. They just do it.

16. Further Development of Market Analysis

In this book, I described a number of tools that the trader can certainly use to scalp very accurately. Although scalping is primarily a mental ability in my eyes, it is worth taking a look at what computer technology has to offer today as additional information.

A. Key Price Levels

It is indisputable that certain price levels of the past few trading days are observed by market participants at the current trading day. Those key levels serve as a kind of orientation to the trader. And depending on the strength or weakness of the actual day these levels act instead as a support or resistance.

The instrument **"Key Price Levels"** is mainly based on three relevant key levels:

- The initial balance (initial range in the future between 08:00 and 09:00 am)

- The equilibrium level of a session

- The value zone of the market

Important levels include:

- Open: opening price of the future

- Close: closing price of the future

- Lower limit of the range of the first hour (initial balance)

- Upper limit of the range of the first hour (initial balance)

- Equilibrium: the densest accumulation of possible price levels

- Lower limit of the value zone (70% of most price quotations)

- Upper limit of the value-zone (70% of most price quotations)

Figure 19: Key Price Levels

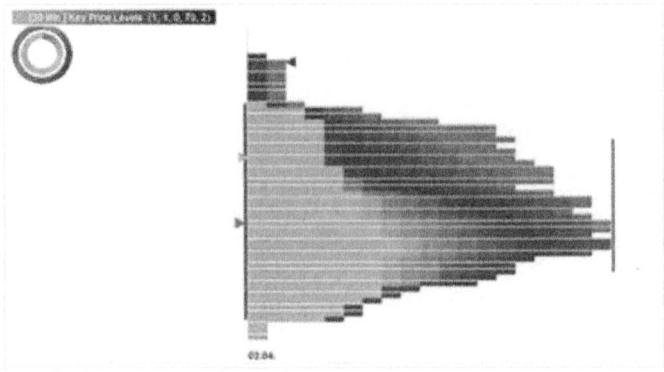

The "Key Price Levels" program calculates all these data automatically and projects the compressed result on the chart. In this way, an evaluation is given based on a Gaussian distribution of yesterday's price quotations (statistical normal distribution or bell curve). The trader receives in this way very valuable information regarding the executed orders of the previous day. Combined with other sources of information, such as histograms or Time & Sales, conclusions on possible trading levels can thus, be made.

B. Live Statistics

In discretionary trading, the trader often chooses "by feel" whether to go long or short. Although certain rules are taken for granted, as is the case for the example in my method, the trading decision is nevertheless based on the "experience" of the trader, on how well he can anticipate future market movements. For some traders, this information is not enough to generate real trading signals. They demand information, based on statistical analysis of a large amount of data from the past. For these traders, the **Live Statistics tool** can be interesting as an additional resource.

Live Statistics determines in real time how often comparable formations have occurred in the past. All past cases are re-analyzed in real time in any situation! Based on this, historical price analysis projections for the current price are shown in the chart.

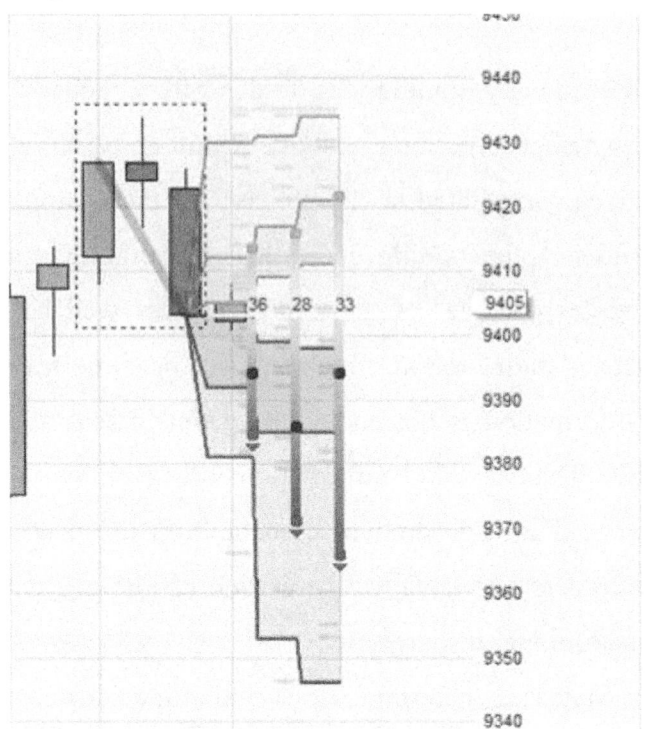

Live Statistics in this example of the mini-DAX future projects possible price levels that the market could reach, based on a number of similar cases in the past. In addition, it also shows how frequently these cases occurred. Thus, the trader has empirical data of the events of the past. The tool cannot predict the future of course, but it provides the trader data with a probability estimate. This is useful in many cases and for various reasons:

- The trader gets a realistic assessment of how far the price could rise over a certain period. This prevents unrealistic expectations regarding the market performance.

- Determination of stop levels and profit targets. These levels will be displayed in the tool.

- The data may confirm or not a signal that a strategy has generated.

Epilogue

I hope, dear reader that with this book I have given you sufficient information on how to scalp the mini DAX future. If you still have questions on this topic, you can reach me at any time via email.

I thank you, dear reader, for buying this book and wish you success in scalping!

Heikin Ashi Trader

pdevaere@yahoo.de

Glossary

Ask: Selling rate

Bid: Demand (purchase price)

Breakeven: Point at which total cost and total revenue are equal

Candlestick: Coding of price changes on the basis of a Japanese analysis technology

Commissions: Costs incurred in the purchase and sale of securities or futures contracts.

Continuation pattern: Break in the main trend, at the conclusion of which the previous direction is resumed.

Contract value: Expressed value of the smallest price change in a future.

Also: value, which refers to an option or a future.

Counter Trend: Countermovement within the main trends

DAX: mainGerman stock index

Doji: Candlestick formation by which the opening and closing prices are at the same level.

Economic Calendar: Calendar with price-sensitive market deadlines.

Entry Strategy: A strategy that determines the entry into a market.

E-Mini Futures: Futures contract on the American index SP500.

Eurex: European Exchange, electronic futures exchange in Frankfurt (Germany), on which German and Swiss futures and options are traded.

Exit Strategy: A strategy that determines the exit from a market.

Expiry date: Expiration of derivative contracts such as futures and options on a derivatives exchange.

Forex: Forex Exchange Market, international currency market.

Futures: Futures contract. Standardized contract to buy or sell a specific amount of a commodity at a specified price, on a specified date.

Gap: A gap between two trading days.

Heikin Ashi: "balancing on one foot" Japanese representation form of price changes.

Indicator: Identification of technical analysis, which is designed to determine price movements of securities.

Limit Order: Order with a fixed price and/or fixed time for the execution.

Linear Stop: A stop order, which is automatically updated each period at a certain distance from the entry price.

Liquidity: Describes the extent to which a security can be sold and bought at any given time.

Long: To be Long; having purchased securities and thus be the owner of the securities.

Margin: Amount of money an investor has to be deposited for the purchase of a futures contract.

Market Maker: Banks or securities firms that take over the obligation to provide for single or multiple securities at any time for a certain minimum of quantities binding buying and selling prices.

Mini Dow: Futures contract on the Dow Jones Industrials Index.

Momentum: The momentum informs the investor about the pace and strength of a price movement.

Multiple Targets: Different price targets for individual contracts.

Opportunity factor: factor, which determines the numbers of trading opportunities are possible within a given period.

Order book: Book, in which all relevant buy and sell orders for the share price are collected. Today it's usually done electronically.

Parabolic stop: The Parabolic Stop moves the activation level from period to period closer to the actual price. This gives it the characteristic parabolic curve.

Payoff Ratio: Ratio of average gains to average loss

Pip: Percentage in point, the smallest change in the price in currency trading.

Rate decision: Describes an announcement of a central bank's decision about the future course of interest rates.

Re-Entry: A second entry in the trade after a failed attempt.

RRR: Risk-reward ratio.

Short position: A trader short is when he sells a position without owning them (short sale).

Slippage: The difference between the estimated and the actual price of an asset purchase.

Spinning Top: Chart pattern with a small body and long shadows.

Spread: The difference between bid and price offer.

Stock index: Measure of the performance of the overall equity market or individual stock groups (e.g. DAX or NASDAQ).

Stop Loss Order: Sell order which is carried out once a certain price is reached.

Tic: The smallest change in price of a futures market.

Time and Sales: Complete overview of all buy and sell orders of a market.

Time Stop: This order automatically closes a position after a set number of periods in advance.

Trailing Stop: An automatic stop loss order.

Trend Following: Trading strategy, this focuses on the following of a once identified trend.

Trend Day: Trading day in the stock market, this is characterized by a clearly identifiable trend.

Underlying: Basic instrument.

Volatility: Standard deviation. Specifies how the price of a market varies

More Books by Heikin Ashi Trader

(Available as e-book and in print)

How to start a Trading Business with $500

Many new traders have little capital available in the beginning, but this is not an obstacle to starting a trading career anyway.

However, this book is not about how to grow a $500 account into a $500,000 account. It is precisely these exaggerated return expectations that bring most beginners to failure.

Instead, the author shows, in a realistic way, how you can become a full-time trader in spite of limited start-up capital. This applies both for traders who want to remain private, as well as for those who want to eventually trade customer funds.

This book shows step by step how to do it. In addition, there is a concrete action plan for each step. Anyone can be a trader in principle, if he or she is willing to learn how this business works.

Contents

About the Author

Heikin Ashi Trader is recognized worldwide as the specialist in scalping with the Heikin Ashi chart. He has been trading this way for 19 years. He traded for a hedge fund and then went into business for himself as a trader. His scalping book "Scalping is Fun!" is an international bestseller and has been sold more than 30,000 times. You can find more information about his scalping method on his website www.heikinashitrader.net

Imprint

Printed in Great Britain
by Amazon

83908723R00058